As Angels of Li

by Steve Wookey*

YOU MIGHT MEET THEM in the Underground, or outside a station or on the street. They will ask you if you would like to join a bible study, or come to a meeting. They will be friendly, but a little insistent. You may already be a member of a church, but somehow their church has so much more to offer, so you really ought to try it out. They will get hold of your telephone number, and then call you often, sometimes each day, to encourage you to come. Before you know it you are caught up with them, You have questions, but somehow you never get the chance to ask them. Your timetable is just too full and the committment expected of you is simply too demanding. You find yourself with a discipler who begins to make all your decisions for you – what job you should do, what course you should take, where you should live. Your parents or friends appear worried by the amount of time that you are spending with the church, so your discipler points out that they are a bad influence, and you ought not to see them too much.

The story of involvement in cults is all too familiar, and yet this time it is a "Christian" church that is involved, and that leaves many questions. Do they not believe the Bible and spend much time studying it? Are they wrong, or just a shade over-zealous? And is it not true that the traditional churches are often compromised and weak by comparison?

This booklet is not written with any desire to cause disunity among Christians, or to make cheap theological points at the expense of another church. I have written because it is my conviction that the Central London Church of Christ (CLCOC), its parent church, the Boston Church of Christ, and all their satellite congregations are seriously and fundamentally wrong in both their theology and their practice. As such I believe they pose a very real danger to those who are already Christians, but who are unsure of their relationship to Christ, and to those who are looking for a faith. I hope that this booklet will be of use both to ministers who are disturbed at finding members of their congregations leaving them for these churches, for Christians similarly worried about friends, and for those who might be tempted to join.

Let is also be said that this booklet is not meant to suggest that there are not many sincere commited Christians within the churches. I personally know of some who have left our fellowship to join CLCOC. It is a sadness because I know them to be genuine followers of Jesus Christ, and in writing this booklet I have no desire to hurt or offend them. But I honestly believe that any commited Christian who stays within the church will suffer from the

---

* Steve Wookey is a Curate on the staff of a large church in central London

1

experience, and my concern is for those who might be tempted to join.

It is also true that there is much within the CLCOC that is a real challenge to the mainline churches. Their commitment, their devotion to the Word of God, and their emphasis on obedience show up areas of weakness in many Christians. We can learn much from their discipline, both in their personal devotional lives and in their evangelism. Their perseverance is in many ways admirable. But this should not blind us to those areas where we believe there are fundamental flaws, and to the errors which are so dangerous.

1. What is the Central London Church of Christ?

The CLCOC is not to be confused with the traditional denomination also known as the Church of Christ. Although they share many of their teachings, they are considerably more extreme and have largely been disowned by that denomination.

The movement traces its roots back to " The Crossroads Church of Christ" in Florida, USA, and to one man in particular, Kip McKean. Converted to Christianity as a student at the University of Florida, and trained within the Crossroads Church himself, McKean finished his studies then tried to start several discipling ministries in other churches.

In June 1979 he arrived in Boston with his wife Elena to set up the Boston Church of Christ, and it was here that he developed with others the techniques and practices that have created such a disturbance. In 1982, teams were sent out to Chicago and London, from where many other offshoots have since sprung. By the Autumn of 1989 there were 67 different centres worldwide with plans for more to come.

In the UK there were, by the same time, congregations in London, Birmingham and Manchester. They have already caused considerable confusion and upset, being banned from certain university and college campuses e.g. The London School of Economics.

2. Who are the leaders?

Initially, the churches looked to a group of Americans for their leadership, but now there are growing up more and more leaders from the areas where the churches are situated. For example, in London the church is now being led by Fred Scott, a young English concert pianist. Nevertheless, the Boston congregation is still seen as the parent church. The leaders seem, for the most part, to be young, highly motivated married couples. The membership of the churches reflect the youth of the leaders.

The driving force behind it all is Kip McKean. Now in his early thirties, McKean was invited to come to Boston to share with people his ideas for discipleship growth. McKean had already aroused considerable opposition by his methods. On one occasion his support at the Memorial Church of Christ in Houston had been terminated because: "...Brother McKean has brought unbiblical practices, peculiar language and subtle, deceitful doctrines to Charleston..." (letter dated April 4 1977 sent to the Heritage Chapel in Charleston, Illinois). Yet it is these same ideas that form the basis for the CLCOC's whole strategy.

Obviously someone of strong personality and conviction, McKean is held in great awe by the different churches:

> *"To say that Kip is a talented man is an understatement and does not do justice to him. Kip is an incredible balance of talent and is leading because of his example in so many areas. There are brothers among us who are known for their humility, or their passion, or their creativity, or their faith. Kip is leading us because he is known for all these virtues and many more. In fact, I cannot think of any virtue that Kip is not known for . There is no greater discipler, disciple, brother, husband, father, leader and friend than Kip McKean...In reality, the Boston Church of Christ happened because someone decided to walk powerfully with God. Kip, we love you, we need you, and we will continue to follow you as you follow Christ."* (From: 'A Decade of Faith, Hope & Love', an article in the COC's magazine Discipleship, Summer 1989)

Other leaders receive similar praise, for example these comments from the same publication about Douglas Arthur, who is now the recognised leader of the Commonwealth churches:

> *"The dynamic growth is a natural extension of a dynamic man of God: Douglas Ray Arthur ... His life is a constant stream of energy, wisdom and concern for others. Whatever fatigue he feels is virtually invisible ... D.A. is really an all-rounder: from sporting endeavours like basketball (Douglas could easily be a professional in England) to more sophisticated games like snooker ... On the intellectual front few can match his quick mind, wit, and way with words. Brilliant at expressing himself ... easy going, fun-loving and his soft blue eyes never reveal a hint of anxiety. "Worry – what is that?" Douglas jests. "Come on, lets flip the frisbee." Yet when he preaches the Word – Watch out! From those same eyes emanate blazing intensity and uncompromising passion for God ... Douglas is a man of God." (From 'The Empire Strikes Back' by Douglas Jacoby , in the same publication as above).*

It needs hardly be said that any group that sets its leaders on such a pedestal is open to great dangers. Leaders cannot be questioned since that reveals a "bad attitude," and their word is final. The right of personal judgement is lost and in its place comes a slavish obedience to the teaching of a few powerful leaders. A brief glance at church history will reveal just how devastating an effect that can have.

As with many authoritarian groups, the hierarchy is very tightly structured. A 'discipler' is given responsibility for each individual, and monitors their 'spiritual growth.' The discipler keeps in constant touch with the person, passing on instructions about all kinds of matters and making all sorts of decisions for them. The discipler is also answerable to someone further up the hierarchy. In such a system an enormous hold is developed over people's lives, and independent thought becomes difficult, if not impossible.

3. What do they believe?

In many ways the movement appears to hold with traditional Protestant teaching. They are correct in their teachings about who Jesus is, the nature of the Trinity, the authority of the Bible. Indeed they resent it when anyone accuses them of not being Christian. When it suits them they will claim to agree with evangelical theology.

However, it is clear from both the nature of their teachings, and the practice of their members that they do not regard members of other churches as being Christians at all. They have claimed to have a policy of not attacking other churches by name, but it is a hollow claim. CLCOC members have attended other churches with the specific intention of inviting people to their own meetings. It has happened on more than one occasion at my own church – indeed once the preacher himself was invited to go! It has been known for members of the CLCOC to be publicly rebuked by their leaders for attending a church service elsewhere.

It must also be said that it is not always easy to understand exactly what they do teach. They have a reluctance to commit anything doctrinal to writing. An American pastor, who has had much contact with the church leaders, comments:
> "As I have met with leaders in the group often times they would say, 'Well, we don't put anything in writing because once you [do], it is man's works... and it quickly degenerates into heresy.'"

From reference works available, however, the main elements of their teaching are as follows:

A. Salvation does not come by faith alone,
"We do not teach that salvation comes by faith alone... it should be noted that "salvation by faith" is in no way identical with "salvation by faith alone".
Douglas Arthur, Letter to UCCF worker16.3.84

B. They teach 5 things as necessary for salvation:

- hear the message, Romans 10. 17
- believe, John 3. 16
- repent, Luke 13.3
- confess Jesus Romans 10.9
- be immersed [from *Guard The Gospel* (Aut, 84)]

C. Baptism is the moment of conversion,

Baptism is very important for the CLCOC. They believe it to be the moment of rebirth when a person becomes a true Christianand receives God's Spirit. Only full immersionis acceptable.

D. Baptism has to be correctly understood.

Baptism is only effective, however, if you believe that it is the moment of conversion. If you think you were a Christian before the baptism, then it is useless. In effect this means that only *their* baptism works, as nobody else shares this understanding. It is only effective if you keep going and do not give up. See Galatians 6.9 and 1 Corinthians 15.2. (Key verses on baptism and conversion for the CLCOC are Acts 2.38; Galatians 3.27; 1 Corinthians 12. 13; Romans 6.4; Acts 22. 16; 1 Peter 3.21; and John 3.5.)

E. Important truths are denied.

The doctrines of Original Sin, Justification by Faith Alone, the Perseverance of the Saints are openly denied. Indeed, one of their publicatins *Guard the Gospel* tells us that "there are literally hundreds of passages which contradict [the doctrine of Once Saved Always Saved]". Holding views different from their teaching is enough to make you a false teacher, and thus an unbeliever. You would need to repent and be baptised.

F. Discipling must be rigorously practised,

Essentially, the framework of the CLCOC system is one of total submission to authority. Any new convert must submit himself to one who is more "mature in the Lord." That submission is almost absolute. Behind this teaching lie two ideas: A disciple is to submit to anything the discipler says unless it violates Scripture; to disobey the discipler is equivalent to not obeying God.

G. The person and work of the Holy Spirit is disregarded

The Holy Spirit is relegated to an 'also ran' in CLCOC theology. He is usually referred to as 'it', and spoken of in terms of being God's personal presence. The Spirit is received when a person is baptised into the church.

The Christian response

What then can one say in answer to these beliefs? I believe it to be defective in the following areas.

A. Salvation

The fundamental question that everyone must ask is this : *how can a person be acceptable to God?* or put another way, *how is someone saved?*

CLCOC teaching
Salvation is by faith and works (including their baptism, claimed to be the moment of conversion). This salvation can be lost if we do not persevere.

The Bible's teaching
Salvation is by God's grace through the death of Jesus Christ on the Cross. This grace becomes ours through faith alone. There is nothing we can do either to earn our salvation or to complete it. We can only accept it as a gift. Ephesians 2 8-9, Titus 3 4-7, Galatians 3 1-4, Romans 3 21-26,

The CLCOC seem to have little understanding of grace. They lay much emphasis on what we do, very little on what God does. They therefore appear to fall into the trap of the oldest heresy of them all – believing that we can gain acceptance with God through our own efforts (*ie Justification by works*). All the emphasis in CLCOC teaching is on what *we* do, not what Christ has already completed for us.

B. Faith and Works.

What is the nature of this saving faith, and what is its relation to works?

CLCOC teaching
Faith of itself is not enough to bring salvation and must be accompanied by certain works. James 2.24 is often quoted as a proof of this teaching.

The Bible's teaching
All that is needed for salvation is faith in Jesus. Saving faith, however, is not just a mental belief, but a personal trust in God, taking Him at His word.

Perhaps a closer look at James 2, 14 onwards will help. First we must grasp the situation James is writing to,(N.B. a fundamental principle of Bible interpretation: first find out what question the writer is trying to answer, before deciding what the passage means). He is not trying to answer the question *"How are we saved?"*, but rather the question *"Given that we are saved by faith, what is saving faith?"* Answer: "it is not just head knowledge, but life-changing heartfelt belief." If we want to answer the other question we would need to look at Romans chapters 1 to 4.

6

Consequently our efforts as Christians are the confirmation that saving faith is present, but **it is faith in Jesus alone that saves us!** Works may indicate saving faith, they do not make saving faith. Ephesians 2.8-10 makes it clear that God's Grace saves through Faith alone (v8), and that works follow (v10) and confirm that saving faith is present. CLCOC teaches the opposite.

C. Baptism.

Baptism is ordained by Jesus, but how should it be practised?

CLCOC Teaching
The church teaches that baptism is the moment of conversion, and has to be understood and practised correctly for it to be effective. It must be adult baptism, and by full immersion, Acts 2.38; Galatians 3. 27; 1 Peter 3. 21.

The Bible's teaching
Although baptism in the New Testament occurs sometimes at the moment of conversion, this is not always the case. From other passages it is clear that all that is needed is faith (Romans 3. 22-25; 4, Galatians 2.16 etc,).

The teaching of the Bible is that we are saved through faith, and that baptism is a public expression that faith is present (Acts 22.16), *but it is not the faith itself.* People could become Christians without being baptised (cf: Luke 23, 42-43), and nowhere is it taught that the only correct expression of faith is baptism. In addition it needs to be said that the CLCOC has no support for its teaching that only baptism with a completely correct understanding of it (i.e. their understanding) is valid . Indeed it drives them to quite ridiculous lengths. One of the leaders in the Boston Church of Christ, Al Baird, was baptised again in 1987, despite already being a leader at the time. Since baptism, in their view, is the moment of conversion presumably he would have to admit that he became a Christian at that point. Other members have been baptised more often still.

D. Assurance.

How can I be sure that I am a Christian and that my sins are forgvien?

CLCOC teaching
Since salvation is not through faith alone, but also involves works, assurance is only possible through having one's commitment checked by the church. When approaching Christians from other churches, their aim is often to undermine assurance by questioning the depth of commitment.

The Bible's teaching
The Bible teaches that assurance is the right of every Christian, based on God's Word (1 John 5, 13), Christ's work (1 Peter 3, 18) and the Spirit's internal and external witness (Romans 8, 16, 1 John 3, 23). Real assurance comes from trusting in God, not in ourselves.

To believe that our obedience is the grounds of our assurance is to risk crushing disappointment and insecurity when failure comes, as it inevitably will. Such teaching leaves people guilt-ridden and without hope.

E. Authority.
What authority can I look to in order to be clear about the truth?

CLCOC teaching
The church claims that the Bible is their only authority. However, in practice, the teaching of the leaders has replaced the Bible's authority. As we shall see, nobody is allowed to question their teaching.

The Bible's teaching
We also accept the authority of the Bible (2 Timothy 3, 16-17). However we do not claim that only our interpretation is correct. Human beings are fallible and can make mistakes. *We* may get it wrong. Only God's Word is infallible, and we must allow anyone to check what is taught by the Word.

Because the CLCOC refuses to allow members that freedom of judgement their authority has ceased to be the Word of God, and become *their teaching on the Word of God* which is very different. Put another way the authority has ceased to be the Bible and has become the movement leaders.
This is of fundamental importance, and explains why the leaders are so concerned to prevent any independent thought. Their whole argument depends on their interpretation being the right one, but in vital areas of biblical understanding it is not. However, nobody is allowed to question them, and this is where the danger lies. The moment we hand over our own responsibility to think, and give it to others, allowing them to interpret what the Scriptures say for us, and then accepting it without further thought, we are on a very slippery slope.

In practice, therefore, the leadership has set itself up as the judge of who belongs to Christ and who does not. But we are warned in the Bible against precisely this sort of attitude (Romans 14.4; 1 Corinthians 4.5).

F. Leadership.
Leaders are placed over us, but what authority should we give their word?

CLCOC teaching
Almost total obedience is required by CLCOC leaders. The only grounds for rejecting a discipler's teaching is if it is against a Biblical command or conscience.

The Bible's teaching
Leaders are to be respected, but their teaching must be checked against the Word of God. In matters where the Word of God is silent individuals have the right to decide for themselves.

Paul states clearly in Romans 14 that in matters where the Bible does not rule absolutely an individual is to follow his own conscience. *"Each should be fully convinced in his own mind" v.4.*

We should take note of Peter's instructions to the leaders in 1 Peter 5. 2-4. Here leadership is seen very clearly as servanthood (note too Mark 10.42-45). Two things must therefore be understood, in which the teaching of the CLCOC on discipling is fundamentally opposed to the teaching of the Bible:

● The Bible teaches that the true leader is a servant, but in the CLCOC he/she has become a tyrant, demanding obedience and determining the lives of members.

● Although the Bible teaches that where the Bible is silent the leader has no right to impose his/her will on an individual, the CLCOC says exactly the reverse: that where the Bible is silent an individual must obey the discipler.

This teaching, and this error is so central to the whole strategy and structure of the church that it must be rightly understood. The idea of a discipler is, although not foreign to the New Testament (for example, Paul and Timothy), certainly very little developed, and in any case totally different to the concept so rigorously applied by the CLCOC.

Conclusions

As a result of these comments I think it is fair to draw the following conclusions:

●At the heart of the CLCOC's teaching is a fundamental misunderstanding of the gospel itself. The gospel tells us that we are saved by grace through faith. The CLCOC tells us that we are saved by works, of which faith is one as are baptism and perseverance. All the emphasis is therefore on us, rather than on Christ.

●Assurance is unlikely, if not impossible.

●The Word of God, seemingly given pride of place by the movement, has in effect been replaced by the teaching of the church. God's Word, however, is all we need, (2 Tim, 3,16)

In its teachings, therefore, the movement is fatally flawed, However it is in the way they treat people that the movement has most obviously caused harm, and it is this that we examine next.

4. How Do They Work?

Many of the classic methods of persuasion used in the cults are present in the techniques use by the CLCOC. If this statement seems unnecessarily harsh consider the following:

Pressure

Underlying much of what the CLCOC do is a great deal of personal and group pressure.

● *Pestering:* Once someone has given a member their name and phone number they are liable to be rung up repeatedly in an effort to persuade them to join the church. Committed Christians, already involved in study groups will nevertheless be pressurised to join this new group. Sometimes it is necessary to be almost abusive before they will stop.

● *Busyness:* Once involved in the church, members' lives are dominated by the busy programme of evangelism, discipling, group study and church. Often students find their work suffering, not out of personal choice but because the leaders expect it.

● *Group Pressure:* Groups are carefully manipulated to put pressure on people to conform. On occasions members are publicly praised or warned to serve as examples to others. On one occasion a member was publicly rebuked for attending another church (*Talking London*, Thames T.V. Jan, 1989). As a result there is a great desire to please among the members. Any criticism of the leaders is immediately regarded as a 'bad attitude'. Leaders, it seems, are always right.

● *Sleep Deprivation:* Members are encouraged to join one of the church houses, where they share rooms (one member lived in a 2-bedroomed house with 12 others) and they get little time to sleep. Often they do not get to bed before midnight, and are expected to be up by 5.30 or 6.0. They get little time to think on their own.

● *Fasting:* Fasting is frequently practised, and is often used as a means of bringing a wayward member to his senses. Through fasting, resistance is lowered, and people are made more open to suggestion.

● *Guilt:* Whenever a member has a question about why the church does or teaches a particular thing the question is almost always turned around on them. The leader will usually refuse to answer saying that the person should get back to the Bible, and will also make the person feel guilty for asking the question. They will be told such things as "I'm disappointed in you for asking the question", "That is not the real problem, the real problem is in you", "That shows a bad attitude," "You're too proud"... It seems that asking

10

any question is wrong. The individual must accept everything which is said without thinking through the rights and wrongs for himself.

Control
The aim of the strong pressure exerted is to establish control over the members. This is aided by the discipling. The relationship with the discipler is very intense. Members are asked to report about all areas of their lives, to confess their sins, and uncritically to accept advice.

'Dating' is encouraged, yet very carefully manipulated. A member is allowed to 'date' once a week, but with a different person. If a boy wishes to go steady, the discipler will speak to the discipler of the girl concerned, If they agree the two are allowed to 'date' once a month initially – with chaperones – then perhaps once a fortnight, until they start thinking about marriage. Effectively members are answerable to their discipler everything. The result is that increasingly people find themselves at the mercy of the church. What the church decides for you is binding. A number of families have been damaged by this, as they have seen their brothers, sisters etc, draw further away, and become incapable of independent action, pawns in the hands of the church leaders. But whenever relatives or friends point this out to members, the discipler will warn against listening to them, using many Bible passages and causing enormous confusion and hurt.

We have already seen the status of the leadership. It need only be added that the whole purpose of the movement seems to be to create an environment where the leader is always right, his word is final, his authority absolute. Of course this makes it extremely hard for anyone to break away.

Deceit
Like many of the cults the CLCOC are not always totally open about what they believe, and have been known to use deceit to gain entry or acceptance. Sometimes they will masquerade as another organisation. At the London School of Economics they called themselves 'The Historical Literature Society', then the 'The Biblical Literature Society".

The North London congregation have recently moved to the Odeon, Swiss Cottage, and have renamed themselves "North London Christian Fellowship", thus inevitably causing confusion and guaranteeing that many will not connect them with the London Church of Christ. Sometimes they will claim to be ordinary Christians doing the same work as others, when in fact they believe that only they are the true church.
> *"It is my sincere desire that there be no quarrelling among those who are sincerely trying to serve Christ in and around London and that a bond of Christian friendship can develop between us all."*
> Douglas Arthur, 1984 to a UCCF worker.

Sometimes the true nature of their belief is covered up. In one of the publications giving instruction about evangelism members are told "don't preach baptism." This is strange, since baptism is a key element in their understanding of conversion.

Indeed in many areas they seem to act in a way counter to Paul's teaching in 2 Corinthians 4.2:

> "Rather we have renounced secret and shameful ways; we do not use deception. nor do we distort the word of God. On the contrary, by setting forth the truth plainly we commend ourselves to every man's conscience in the sight of God."

The upshot of all this is that the CLCOC appears increasingly like a cult with all the associated dangers. It is no exaggeration to say that many who have been involved with the church for any length of time find themselves quite severely disturbed. They have difficulty in making decisions, shaking off feelings of guilt, and coming to terms with life outside.

5. Why do they attract so many followers?

It is unquestionably true that the CLCOC, and other churches of the same movement are growing fast. Indeed statistics are, for them, a test of the truth of their teaching and approach. Much is made of the fact that they are a growing church, whereas other churches are shrinking. They are not the only religious group to experience growth, however. The rapid growth of Islam, or Mormonism, does not make them true. But given their undoubted numerical growth what explanations can we offer? What sort of people do they attract?

Zealous Christians

They appeal to young Christians who are frustrated by the apparent apathy of so many within the ordinary Christian churches. In a sermon entitled "How is this church different?" Douglas Arthur states that the difference between themselves and evangelical Christians as being commitment. They are, he claims, 95% committed, whereas evangelical churches are 5% committed.

Of course we too want to encourage commitment, and we are challenged by the commitment shown by those within the CLCOC. Indeed we accept that many of the problems within Christian churches stem from a half-hearted response to the love of God shown to us in Christ. But a similar devotion to their beliefs is shown by certain Moonies and Communists. Commitment to a particular cause does not make it true. People can be sincerely wrong. So although the CLCOC is attractive to many for this reason, they should first consider whether what is being taught is the truth as revealed in the Bible.

The Vulnerable

They prey on people who are vulnerable, or going through a crisis . It is interesting to note how young the congregations tend to be, and how many overseas people there are. In the middle of big cities, which is where their efforts are targeted, people tend to be more vulnerable, and open to anyone offering friendship, without stopping to ask where the truth lies.
This is true of so many religious groups and sometimes of mainstream churches. Christians must beware of bulldozing people into belief. If we believe that it is God who converts people through the Holy Spirit, then we must allow them the time and space to think for themselves. If you are looking for the truth yourself, you must never allow anyone to push you into anything without first finding out what is involved.

The Uncertain

They are attractive to those who are unsure in their faith, and want certainties. There is a tremendous amount of guilt inducement, and in that guilt they claim to have the clear answer. In addition it is comforting not to have to think, but be able to leave it all up to another. It seems to offer an easy way. But do not be fooled. They may claim to offer certainty, but will not be able to deliver it. Any way of salvation that relies on our own efforts can never give assurance. The only sure hope of forgiveness and acceptance by God lies in the Cross of Christ.

The Untaught

For those who have no clear understanding of what the Christian faith is, there is an immediate attraction. These people are friendly, young, lively and sincere. They seem to be Christians, yet are so much more fun than ordinary churchgoers. How can they be wrong?

Indeed many people within the CLCOC are true Christians. But that does not make their teaching trustworthy. It is a false gospel that they preach, however close to the real one, and it must be recognised as such. If you are unsure yourself what is the truth look for other Christians, trained in the Bible, who will be able to explain the Bible's message, the message of Jesus Christ in whom *"God was reconciling the world to himself, not counting people's sins against them"* (2 Corinthians 5.19). False teachers, after all, are inclined to masquerade as angels of light. (See 2 Corinthians 11. 13-15)

6. What Should Our Response Be?

Being so close to mainstream Christianity, and yet at the same time being so distinct, the CLCOC can be very hard to combat. We may have no desire to cause division amongst Christians, and hate the thought of allowing the Christian Church to be seen by the world as being divided against itself, but still know that we must do something. We need to consider our reaction to them as a church, and then our reaction to people who are involved.

Advice to Church Leaders

We must pray: If we believe that their teaching is seriously at fault, and destructive to those involved, we must recognise that it is a spiritual battle that we are involved in. We must pray that those involved will realise that what they are hearing is not the right interpretation of the Bible.

We must be clear in our own teaching/understanding: One of the reasons that groups such as the CLCOC are flourishing is because of the lack of good teaching within so many of our churches. The error of the CLCOC's teaching is not easy to discern, but it is even harder for those who have not been taught Christian fundamentals. Those who have been trained and grounded in such principles as *'sola fide'* (justification by grace through faith alone), and *'sola scriptura'* (the Bible as our only authority) will recognise false teaching much more easily than those whose diet has tended to be of a more experiential kind.

It follows that those who teach have a real responsibility to explain clearly the traditional truths of the gospel. If the CLCOC is operating in your area it will be necessary to warn your church in love against them. Do not assume that because you have had no contact with them that your congregation has not. On the occasions when we have publicly warned against them, we have been suprised by the size of the comeback.

We must realise that severe psychological damage can be caused in those caught up in the movement for any length of time: They can find it very hard to adjust again to society after they have been used to having all their decisions made for them. There are organisations with great experience of helping those coming out of the cults, and we may well need to use them.

Advice For Those With Friends in the Church

We need to be prayerful: False teaching is always a threat to the church, and we need to ask God to protect his people. Pray for your friends.

We need to be securely grounded ourselves: One of the main tricks of the CLCOC is to attack the beliefs and assurance of ordinary Christians. If you have a friend with the church he/she will be told that you are not a Christian because you are not committed enough, because you have not been baptised by them, because you do not evangelise etc. It can be extremely disturbing. You must therefore be clear about your own salvation and have a clear understanding of the gospel. (1 Peter 3.15).

We need to be informed: Half-baked and ill-informed prejudice against the CLCOC will not help our friends, but will only drive them further away. If the CLCOC can show that there is no truth in our allegations their cause is only helped. Try to understand what they teach and how they work. One

14

former member said that the reason he had to listen to his family when they questioned him about his involvement with the church was that they knew so much about it. Many of the criticisms they will make of your own church may be true: lack of love, no evangelistic zeal, boring etc. **This does not mean that their church is right!**

We need to be sensitive: The same person also said that when he was prepared to allow himself to be tackled about his membership of the church, it took him an hour to realise that something was very wrong, but three days (of intensive discussion) to admit it. Many church members have given up a great deal in their zeal, and it can be extremely humbling to admit that they have been mistaken.

Remember too that members will come under intense pressure from the church if they show signs of wanting to leave. They will be told that they will go to hell, that they will have no hope etc,. and it can be very distressing for them. They will also be told not to speak to other Christians.

We need to be patient: It may take time to show our friends, or for them to realise for themselves, that the CLCOC is seriously mistaken. In the meantime do not give up, and do not withdraw friendship. There is a very high turnover rate in the church, and though many join, many also leave. Remember too that it may be useless to engage in endless theological arguments. In all probability it will cause more barriers to be raised. Love, patience and the odd question that shows a true understanding of what goes on will produce more results in the long-term. The more it becomes a personal battle, the harder it will be for someone to admit they are wrong.

Advice For Those Involved In The Church

If you are already a member it will be obvious that I have serious questions about the nature and teaching of the church. You may well be unconvinced. But at least consider the following points. If the church is teaching the truth, then you having nothing to lose. If it is not, then you have everything to gain.

Be prepared to ask serious questions: Do not allow your questions to go unanswered. If you cannot understand something that is being taught, ask about it. If they say you are wrong to question, refer them to passages in the Bible where it was considered absolutely right to enquire further.
Look at the example of the Bereans in Acts 17. 10-12. They had to find out themselves if what Paul said was true. Read 1 Thessalonians 5.20; and Galatians 1. 6-10. Paul did not claim for himself that he would always be right, but asked his friends to check what he said by the Bible. It is the Bible that is authoritative, not the church leaders.

Take your own notes on what is taught: The CLCOC may tell you that you cannot take your own notes, but do not accept that. You have the right and the responsibility to understand the Bible's message. When you get home read the verses you have been given in their context. Do they mean what you have been told they mean?

Avoid moving in to one of their houses: The aim of their communal houses is to keep a closer watch upon you. You are a free agent, and they have no right to insist on this. If you do move in with members of the church it will be very hard for you to get time or space to think for yourself.

Find out all you can about the church: The church has been accused of certain malpractices, such as using techniques that are typical of cults. Is there any truth in these accusations? What of the leaders? How many times have they been baptised? Why has the church been labelled an "insidious cult" by the mainline Church of Christ? (Talking London Jan, 89). If the church is demanding your total allegiance, you need to find out all you can about it.

Key Verses

Don't be put off by their proof texts: Look at the context and show them you understand the verses better. Beware – arguing over texts can be unproductive. Here are some pointers on CLCOC proof texts:

Acts 2.38: Out of context this could mean that you need to be baptised to be saved. But look at 2.21 and 3.19 – no mention of baptism.

1 Peter 3.21: Baptism now saves you! But corresponding to what? To the flood. The ark (Jesus) saves not the water. It is faith in Jesus that saves.

Mark 16.16: Condemnation comes through not believing, not because baptism is rejected.

Acts 22.16: Sins not washed away until baptised? Not what the Lord told Ananias – see Acts 9.17 BROTHER Saul! Already converted before baptism.

Matthew 28.18: Make disciples and *then* baptise.

1 Corinthians 1.17: Paul not sent to baptise, but to preach the gospel!

Acts 16.31: Believe in Christ and then be baptised.

!Corinthians 15.1-5: The Gospel – no mention of baptism, only Jesus.

Philippians 2.12: We do not work towards salvation, but work out the salvation already received. NB v 13 God is at work in you – not our work.

Matthew 24.13: Endure and be saved. But compare the Luke 21.18-19 parallel. We may lose physical life, but not spiritual.

Further help

Further help is available from: Reachout Trust. P.O.Box 43 Twickenham TW2 7EG.

16

An Ex-Member writes

I was doing well in my studies and having a great time socially at University, but, like many people, I was searching for some sort of spiritual reality in my life.

Towards the end of my first year, a friend – a bright, attractive and friendly person – invited me to his church for a Sunday service. I thought I would go, as I fancied myself as being open and experimental. After the service, he suggested we study the Bible together, and I then met with him regularly, as well as going to the Church on Sundays and to other mid-week meetings. The people impressed me with their strict sense of morality, conviction about the Bible and their committment. It was challenging to my own habits and ideas.

Although other people had warned me about the strict 'fundamentalism' of this group, and that it was rumoured to be a cult, my friend was urgent and insistent about our meeting together to study, and so I continued to meet with him. He showed me such care and love that it was hard to say no.

Eventually, because I became convinced that the teachings were true, I was baptised and became a member. For months I kept the baptism a secret from my family.

Soon after I was baptised, I discovered that many of the Church Church meetings were compulsory. On one Saturday evening, the church was having a concert. I opted not to go because I needed to study for an exam. I was challenged about this by a fellow student who was a leader, and discovered that not only were the special events mandatory, but so were the retreats, evangelism, morning quiet times, bible discussions, conferences, seminars, sector meetings and, of course, financial contributions. In London, members must pledge the amount they are to give, and are held accountable for it. They are followed up regularly by their disciplers for "special Mission Contributions." I was encouraged to move into a flat with another member.

Whenever I questioned these things, the following responses were most commonly given: "That's not the issue – the issue is that you're not broken," "It's in the Bible," "I'm disappointed in you, how could you be questioning now?" or "Brother, you just need to change."

My friend became my Discipler, and we met one to three times a week. I was told to imitate him, and be submissive to him. Using the example of King David's Mighty Men, an Evangelist once told us that we were to display "Wierd Loyalty" to our disciplers.

After being baptised a second time (because I did not repent properly the first time), I became a discipler myself. We had to invite between one and five people a day, and get as many phone numbers as possible.I was encouraged to reach out to sharp or open people who could become future leaders.

As my intensity and involvement grew, my grades at university fell sharply. I had no time for non-Christian friends. My sense of humour vanished. When challenged on these things by my friends and family, I viewed their remarks as Satanic.

I was not happy in the Church. My discipler would constantly re-assure me that if I would evangelise more it would all become clear to me. At that time I believed that the only alternative to being a part of the group was going to Hell.

My parents called in cult specialists who knew about the group and who challenged me on its teachings. After 5 minutes talking with them, I knew that something was seriously wrong – but it took me three days of argument to admit that the Church was seriously wrong in its teaching and practice. I left soon afterwards.

Had I not been 'exit counselled' by these cult specialists, I would have spent years more in the Church – perhaps the rest of my life.

Although, in many ways, I owe my faith in Christ to the Church, membership was a bad experience and I would encourage anyone involved to leave.

There is a new group on the British Christian landscape. Fast growing, highly committed and fearless in street evangelism - they put many traditional evangelical churches to shame.

And yet there are grounds for serious concern over both their theology and the techniques they use to achieve their 'success'.

This balanced but uncompromising critique of the Central London Church of Christ and its offshoots measures their teaching and practice against the standards of Scripture.

The booklet is written by Steve Wookey, Curate on the staff of a central London church on whose doorstep the CLCOC was based during the 1980's. He has had dealings with members and ex-members in recent years.

Published by The Narrowgate Press
ISBN: 1 873166 00 1